DEMYSTIFYING COLLEGE SUCCESS

45 TIPS
To Skyrocket Your Success from College and Beyond!

"Larry M. Jacobson goes above and beyond to enlighten and empower his audiences as an interview guest, speaker, or presenter."

~ Zeb Welborn
President of Welborn Media and Host of Defining Success Podcast

LARRY M. JACOBSON, MBA, Ed.D

WHAT OTHERS ARE SAYING...

"*Larry was able to give us motivational and organizational pointers that I still use today. He would meet with a group of students, each time I gained something new/different from the time before.*"

~ **Amy Taylor**
J.D. Candidate, The John Marshall Law School

"*I have had the opportunity to bring Larry in to speak with students and he always leaves the room inspired and ready to approach the next hurdle with a new energy and from new perspective. Larry captivates his audiences with entertaining tales from his own life and successes and leaves them enthused about capitalizing on the opportunities in their lives.*"

~ **Brandon O'Leary**
Executive Director, Management Advisory Services
at Indiana University Foundation

"*I was lucky to meet Larry after he gave a speech to my Music Industry class during Freshman Year at Indiana University. Larry's ability to extend his extensive knowledge to students is extremely effective and motivating.*"

~ **Nishi Tomar**
Digital Strategy Intern at Initiative

"*One of the constant themes in Dr. Jacobson's life has been the desire to have a positive impact on others, and his book is the embodiment of this goal.*"

~ **Vincent Freda**
Chief Operating Officer of Isolation Network,
Parent Company of INgrooves

"I attended Larry's speech and Q&A session more than one time. The information he shared including his own long-term professional experience in executive positions, tips on career development and etc. was wise, inspiring, thought-provoking, and very meaningful to us. I still keep pages of the notes I took on his guest lecture and benefited from them in my career."

~ Yiting Liang
Touring Intern at AEG Live

"I was responsible for finding a strong keynote speaker for the Scholarship Dinner on Friday Night. I immediately thought of Larry Jacobson, whom I had known since college when we were both involved in Union Board. Larry could show students and alumni alike how Union Board advanced his career in music and lead him to be a Vice President at a major music label in Los Angeles. Not only was Larry able to tell that story, but did so in a way that was humorous, engaging and inspiring to those students — and left a lasting impression and passion in their minds. I received several compliments from alumni regarding Larry's remarks, and I hope that Larry can speak again at future events."

~ Christian Carroll
Account Manager, North America, Europe & Asia
at Lienau Sales & Marketing

"Larry is an amazing person that I've had the pleasure of meeting in my time at Indiana University. His positive attitude has helped influence myself, as well as many other students, to pursue their dreams and live positively. He's the guy you want to follow, because he'll show you how to lead."

~ Brooke McElyea
National Sales Account Coordinator at Tribune Company

"Most students have no idea how to prepare for their financial future and are left in the dark. Larry's mission has been to educate, inspire and motivate others to plan more for their financial future and his commitment to his cause is unparalleled. Larry M. Jacobson goes above and beyond to enlighten and empower his audiences as an interview guest, speaker, or presenter. I'm always impressed with his desire to serve others."

~ **Zeb Welborn**
President at Welborn Media and Host of
Defining Success Podcast

"I would recommend to anyone who wants to become successful they take a page from the Larry M. Jacobson playbook, starting with an unbreakable positive attitude, crystal clear organizational skills, and the desire to attract wealth through personal effort."

~ **Todd Davis**
Senior Trading Instructor, Online Trading Academy

"Larry M. Jacobson is one of the finest professional resources I know. I have interviewed hundreds of his peers; Larry is a First Among Peers. He has unusually great insight and he cleverly connects various aspects of life. Larry applies all of that to his teaching and 1:1 coaching. I highly regard Larry M. Jacobson."

~ **Reese Woolf, Ph.D**
Best-selling author of Executive Speaking In a Weekend

DEMYSTIFYING
COLLEGE SUCCESS

45 TIPS
to Skyrocket Your Success
from College and Beyond!

Larry M. Jacobson, MBA, Ed.D

T.I.M.E.
INSTITUTE LLC
Los Angeles

Copyright © 2014 by Larry M. Jacobson, MBA, Ed.D.

For permission requests, write to the publisher, addressed "Attention: Permissions Coordinator," at the address below.

T.I.M.E. Institute LLC
1107 Fair Oaks Avenue #141
South Pasadena, CA 91030
www.TIMEInstituteLLC.com

Layout / Cover Design and Copyediting by Kate Sancer Jacobson

Ordering Information:
Quantity sales — special discounts are available on quantity purchases by corporations, associations, and others.
For details, contact the "Special Sales Department" at the address above.

Printed in the United States of America

Jacobson, Larry M.
    DEMYSTIFYING COLLEGE SUCCESS: 45 TIPS to Skyrocket Your Success from College and Beyond! / by Larry M. Jacobson, MBA, Ed.D — 1st ed.

Library of Congress Control Number: 2014914645

ISBN 978-0-9910803-2-8

Warning – Disclaimer
The purpose of this book is to educate and provide helpful and informative material of a general nature on the subject matter covered. The author may have used the names of friends, mentors, and/or associates, and such usage should be interpreted neither as an endorsement, nor a disparagement. Any perceived slights against people or organizations are entirely unintentional. The author or publisher does not guarantee that anyone following the techniques, suggestions, tips, ideas, or strategies will become successful as each person is ultimately responsible for his or her own successes and failures. Accordingly, the use of the materials and information in this publication shall be at your own risk. The author and publisher shall bear neither liability, nor responsibility, to anyone with respect to any loss or damage caused, or alleged to be caused, either directly or indirectly by the information contained in this book.

ACKNOWLEDGMENTS

WE ALL SUCCEED based upon surrounding ourselves with the right people and circumstances.

I consider myself very fortunate to have friends, family, business associates, and last, but not least, *students* who make this my reality and continually inspire me to be my best.

I humbly dedicate this book to all of my students who are truly my teachers. You help me grow and improve every single time I'm fortunate enough to stand in front of you.

ABOUT LARRY M. JACOBSON

IN HIS EARLIER life, Larry had a 22-year career as a music entertainment industry executive for the world's largest music and publishing company, was a professional on-air radio personality, is a guest speaker at major colleges and universities, and has completed four academic degrees in music and business (which includes a Doctor of Education degree in organizational leadership and an MBA).

In 2014, Larry released the quintessential "How-to guide" that he wished he had been handed back when he was in high school and college — *Demystifying Success: Success Tools and Secrets They Don't Teach You in High School.* Since it has been so well-received, Larry was inspired to continue his mission in helping young adults make their way through college and into the "real world," following it up with *DEMYSTIFYING COLLEGE SUCCESS: 45 TIPS to Skyrocket Your Success from College and Beyond!*

As a dynamic speaker who understands what it takes to reach his audiences, Larry generously shares his personal life-lessons and principles gleaned through his own accomplishments and mistakes in his career, relationships, and in business to inspire college students to achieve the success they desire.

Motivate and Inspire Others!
"Share this Book"

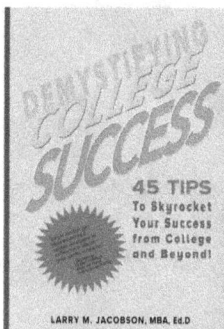

DEMYSTIFYING COLLEGE SUCCESS: 45 TIPS to Skyrocket Your Success from College and Beyond!

Everyone needs some inspirational guidance now and then. In his accessible voice, Larry shares practical and actionable tips to give college students a jumpstart on achieving their success.

While these insightful tips are truly helpful for college students to use, they really can be applied to anyone, of any age. It's never too late to grow, change, and improve your life to achieve the success you desire! **$12.00**

Special Quantity Discounts

3 – 20 Books	$10.00 each
21 – 99 Books	$9.00 each
100 – 499 Books	$8.00 each
500 – 999 Books	$7.00 each
1000+ Books	$6.00 each

CONTENTS

Mentors

{Tips 1 – 3}

WE CANNOT TEACH
PEOPLE ANYTHING,
WE CAN ONLY HELP
THEM DISCOVER IT
WITHIN THEMSELVES.

~ GALILEO

I HAVE FOUND that mentors serve as excellent role models, sounding boards, and can truly help you in achieving your desired goals. They not only model the way for your potential success, but they can also serve as great resources for information and advice.

To this day, I continue to hold my mentors in high esteem, feel gratitude for their supportive guidance, and maintain relationships with many of them.

While I have learned so much at this point in my life — which I have been compelled to impart to you here — by no means do I think my personal work is done.

We are all works in progress.

I strongly believe that no matter how much success one achieves, it's vitally important to always pursue continued growth and improvement. I also believe this pursuit should be a lifelong endeavor that fosters an inspired, and inspiring, life.

You can reach out to anyone you consider a role model (teachers, parents, siblings, professionals, others) for encouragement, guidance, and advice.

Your potential mentor should be someone whom you look up to and is willing and committed to take the time to assist you toward accomplishing your interests, goals, and passions.

Barring any time constraints, most people will usually be flattered when asked to be a mentor. It is a great opportunity for potential mentors to give back. Especially if they, too, were the recipients of positive mentoring in the past.

TIP 1 | REACH OUT TO YOUR ROLE MODELS FOR ADVICE

If you can't find a personal mentor to work with you, don't be afraid to reach out via email or letters inquiring about guidance or advice from other role models you find inspirational.

What's the worst thing that could happen...that your chosen mentor is either too busy, or does not feel comfortable addressing your requests? Most often, if you are thorough in researching them in advance, and you politely and succinctly reach out for guidance, you may just be pleasantly surprised by their willingness to take on that role.

Beyond researching people you plan to reach out to, I also strongly encourage you research role models who inspire you. You can readily read, watch, and study authors, experts, and others that interest you to acquire information, lessons, and strategies to help you further your own creative talents, knowledge, and goals.

TIP 2 | RESEARCH AND REACH OUT TO INSPIRATIONAL ROLE MODELS

Although it may not be feasible for you to create a personal mentoring relationship with certain people, you can still gain a lot by admiring and learning from them when you research their accomplishments and experiences.

Identify three potential inspirational role models you would like to research and reach out to for inspiration and guidance:

1 _____

_____

2 _____

_____

3 _____

_____

Take a few moments to ask yourself how a mentor would personally benefit you at this time in your life.

After you have identified three potential mentors you would like to approach for support and guidance, detail why you think these people would be good role models:

1 _____

_____

2 _____

_____

3 _____

_____

If you do not have the time to research and reach out to inspirational role models, or don't yet feel comfortable approaching others to serve as your personal mentors, then I suggest you simply look around and observe.

Be open to choosing someone who inspires you, whom you may model yourself after — a close friend, classmate, co-worker, or someone else you truly admire.

Use the next couple of pages to write down their positive qualities that most inspire you and that you wish to emulate and then add details about *why* you wish to emulate them.

TIP 3

"IMMITATION IS
THE SINCEREST
FORM OF
FLATTERY"
~ CHARLES CALEB
COLTON

If you're committed to start incorporating these positive traits into your daily routines, you may be surprised by how quickly they become your own regular habits.

1 |

2 |

3 |

4 |

5 |

6 _____

_____

7 _____

_____

8 _____

_____

How will you plan to incorporate these inspiring
qualities into your everyday life?

**Make them your habits...
TAKE ACTION!**

Network,
Network,
Network

{Tips 4 – 10}

THE RICHEST PEOPLE IN
THE WORLD LOOK FOR
AND BUILD NETWORKS,
EVERYBODY *ELSE* LOOKS
FOR WORK.

~ ROBERT KIYOSAKI

NO ONE WHO was ever truly successful in life accomplished their goals alone. If you ask anyone who has ever risen to the top of their field or profession, they will most likely tell you: "It's who you know, your connections, along with tons of hard work that helps you to get where you want to go."

Their strategy is simple and you can readily adopt it yourself: seek out other people who can help further your goals. This is why it is extremely important that you "network, network, network," from an early age and beyond, so that you can build a strong affiliation of personal and professional contacts/relationships which can help you to grow your future success.

If you recently moved to a new city for school or work, or you are introverted and simply do not feel comfortable approaching new people, consider joining a club or professional organization to meet other like-minded people that share the same interests as you.

Don't be shy — take advantage of any opportunity that will allow you to practice meeting and speaking with other people. In time, as with any practice, your confidence will increase as you become more comfortable meeting and networking with new people.

When you truly know yourself — the <u>real</u> you — you will feel confident enough to ride out any awkward discomfort that may arise when beginning to network with others.

Being authentic and sincere throughout all of your interactions goes a long way toward making it easier for others to forge an honest connect with you. This connection is key in leading to the mutually beneficial personal and/or professional relationships you should be striving for while networking.

TIP 4 | BE YOURSELF!

If you are interested in finding out how others really perceive you, I have an exercise that should help you gain some clarity and perspective to assess that. Choose five close friends (that you really trust and respect), and ask them to *type* (not write) five things that they really like about you, and five things that they wish you would change about yourself, and ask them to return their answers to you anonymously.

By requesting anonymous replies, your friends will be inclined to be more honest with you about their responses because they'll feel like they're dodging hurting your feelings. Stay objective while reading your valuable feedback and embrace the lessons you learn from the exercise.

Whenever you attend a social or professional event or function, try to engage with other people outside of your "normal" comfort zone.

Make it a goal to try to reach out and speak with new people that you would not normally get an opportunity to meet with.

After the event, it is extremely important that you follow up with a quick email if you liked engaging with that new person. But most importantly, create a "call to action" when you reach out to them.

Basically, a call to action is when you give the other person an opportunity to respond in a way that will move the relationship forward. Suggest a time to speak on the phone, or meet for coffee, lunch, dinner, etc.

TIP 5 | EXPLORE BEYOND YOUR COMFORT ZONE

Figure out if there are ways that you can assist this new contact in the future that would help you to forge a new personal and/or professional relationship.

In other words, you want to establish a mutually beneficial relationship.

The next time you are at a networking event or function, give yourself a goal to meet and speak with five new people. Then immediately write down any pertinent information on the back of their business cards so you can reference it later.

Below, list those people and write down any details about your interaction that you wrote down on the back of their business cards.

1 _____

2 _____

3 _____

4 _____

5 _____

What will your calls to action be?

Your social network can include people that you meet at various events: school, social, or business. They can be members of clubs, groups, or organizations that you choose to join, or they can be people that you connect with through various social media sites (LinkedIn, Facebook, Twitter, etc.) who share similar interests or goals.

Try to expand your social network by reaching out to new contacts via LinkedIn, Facebook, Twitter, etc. Ask your current social media contacts if they can introduce, or recommend you to someone else online with whom you would really like to connect to/ affiliate with.

TIP 6 | ESTABLISH SOCIAL CONNECTIONS

GROWING YOUR NETWORK:

On LinkedIn and Twitter, accept everyone that wants to connect with you (you never know how they might help you in the future). Send your prospective connection a message that gives them a good reason (incentive) to connect with you, and make sure to include a call to action that they do so.

Some approaches you could use are:

- "I met you at…or from…or I saw your profile through…"

- "You came up on LinkedIn when I was searching for…" (Put your future relationship into context for them.)

- "I would like to get you on the phone to talk about…"

- Or let them know through email what you'd like to discuss (what do you want from them?)…"Can we jump on a call?" "When is a good time to talk?" (Don't forget to provide your email and phone number.)

First impressions *do* matter, so always project a positive self-image because you never know who you might meet or be introduced to.

In social or professional situations, always dress in alignment with the way you want others to perceive, identify, and/or remember you.

Dress for Success — your clothes, accessories, grooming, etc. should reflect the brand that you wish to project to the world (both in person and online).

Maximize your social media presence on: Facebook, Twitter, LinkedIn, Pinterest, etc. — share your professional message and goals

TIP 7 | OWN YOUR PERSONAL BRAND

through social media. Make sure you do not overlook establishing a simple, yet professional-looking online presence with your own website. If you haven't already done this, just follow these six simple steps and you should be good to go:

1. Purchase a personal URL website address with your brand name (i.e., your name – e.g., www.LarryMJacobson.com)

2. Create a free blog page (WordPress, Blogger, etc.)

3. Select all and copy your new blog's URL

4. Go to the site where you purchased your URL (where it's "parked")

5. Find the forwarding feature and paste the copy of your blog's link and "mask" it

6. Give it a little time to update and test that when your "brand name" URL is typed into the browser, the masked forwarding feature is enabled properly and it rolls over to your blog (new personalized website)

Then when your new contacts looks you up, they won't see just a blog, they'll see only your "brand name" URL address and you will have professionally presented yourself while also demonstrating how you pay attention to details!

Act appropriately in all personal and business situations — you never know who's watching/listening.

- Carry business cards to all networking events — they should always reflect your brand and personal message

- Include your new personal website on your business card where they will find a downloadable PDF of your resume ("CV")

Networking is all about meeting new people and building mutually beneficial relationships. You can't learn from others if you are constantly the only one doing the talking.

You need to listen and provide the other person space to speak, answer, and share their own thoughts and opinions so that you can both connect with each other to determine if you can build a personal and/or professional relationship for the future.

To ensure you are providing good reciprocity, look for opportunities to get the other person to talk about themselves or their ideas.

TIP 8 | DON'T BE THE SMARTEST PERSON IN THE ROOM

Ask them questions that do not simply require a "yes" or "no" answer.

Here are five "opener" suggestions:

1. "What do you do and how did you get started in your current job or career?"

2. "What were your goals for attending this function?"

3. "How did you hear about this event?"

4. "What are some of the biggest opportunities or challenges you foresee in the future of your industry, company, school, organization, etc.?"

5. "Have you had a lot of success networking with other people at these types of events?"

Remember, people love to talk about themselves and will be more open to associating with people who love to listen to them.

Give your conversations enough time to grow organically while getting to know the interests and goals of the people with whom you choose to network at your functions.

Take mental notes of the information the other people share with you to determine if you can help them, or provide them with any value after the networking event.

Be aware of when the conversation starts to wind down and that it's time to move on. Then ask the other person if it would be okay to follow up with them at a later time to continue your conversation.

TIP 9 | NEVER OVERSTAY YOUR WELCOME

You do not want to monopolize the other person's time, "holding them hostage" by cornering them and suffocating them with uncomfortable conversation.

Create a call to action that you can confirm with the other person (email, phone call, etc.) so you can follow up with them after the event at a specific date and time.

Remember, your goal at a networking event is to acquire information to determine if you can possibly cultivate personal and/or professional relationships with others at the event based upon providing each other with valuable resources and potential referrals.

You are not there to "pitch" them your products or services. If you effectively network and build good relationships, there will be plenty of time in the future to exchange ideas, etc.

No one likes to feel cornered like their backs are up against the wall. If you are attending a social event, keep things light and festive. If you are attending a business or professional function, keep the previously suggested opener questions in mind. Inquire as to why they are attending and what they hope to gain out of participating, etc. Be prepared to answer the same kinds of questions.

TIP 10 | PITCH YOURSELF, NOT YOUR PRODUCTS

You also want to request your new contact's business card. Once you've parted ways, pause to write down as many things as you can remember about that person on the back of their card (hobbies, goals, personal details, etc.) so that you can refer to this information prior to your follow up.

In addition, go online and research the individual to learn more about them, their company, interests, etc. The information you gather will serve as potential talking points during your future encounters.

Create three potential networking talking points about yourself when approaching others at an event (be sure to avoid sounding like a salesperson):

1 _____

_____

2 _____

_____

3 _____

_____

WATCH YOUR THOUGHTS; THEY BECOME WORDS. WATCH YOUR WORDS; THEY BECOME ACTIONS. WATCH YOUR ACTIONS; THEY BECOME HABITS. WATCH YOUR HABITS; THEY BECOME CHARACTER. WATCH YOUR CHARACTER; IT BECOMES YOUR DESTINY.

~ LAO TZU
(CHINESE TAO PHILOSOPHER)

Healthy Personal Relationships

{Tips 11 – 14}

IF YOU AIN'T LOSING FRIENDS, YOU AIN'T GROWING UP.

~ SNOOP DOG

YOUR THOUGHTS, EMOTIONS, and the people with whom you choose to surround yourself largely determine how well you protect and nurture your ability to achieve success.

Surrounding yourself with the right people not only impacts your overall confidence and self-esteem, but these same people actually impact your overall ability to make good decisions — the key path to creating your *probable* (vs. possible) outcomes for success.

Have you ever noticed that depending on the state of our emotional well-being and/or self-perception, for better or worse we tend to attract certain types of people into our lives?

Many people fail to realize how important it is to be able to quickly identify and protect themselves from people who pretend to have their best interests at heart.

When they aren't in a healthy emotional state, their ability to spot disruptive, self-loathing individuals is greatly diminished. This lack of awareness is so detrimental to achieving their success.

Successful healthy people, on the other hand, are acutely aware of these unhealthy individuals and their negative intentions.

And as a result, they learn how to co-exist, maneuver around, or completely avoid them altogether in order to protect themselves from any of their sabotaging behavior.

Unfortunately, during one's lifetime it is all too easy to come across master emotional manipulators. These unhealthy individuals study and befriend their unwitting targets and very quickly learn how to make them feel comfortable in their presence. They are extremely skilled at telling people what they want to hear, pretending to like the things they like, or even worse, fostering a false sense of a security within the relationship to ensure that their victim will take their bait.

The only problem is that their actions are not sustainable over time because they are not being authentic with their targets. They are simply

TIP 11 | THE BAIT AND SWITCH

trying to get them to trust and/or fall in love with them as a means to an end — to satisfy their own needs.

News Flash:
These emotional parasites have an agenda!

So how does one effectively address and counteract the emotional parasite's bait and switch agenda?

PUT THEIR WORDS ON MUTE AND STUDY THEIR ACTIONS!

If they say something that strikes you as manipulative and inconsistent with their actions, immediately confront them on these inconsistencies. If they become defensive with you, you have clearly unearthed a chink in their deceptive armor.

If this uncomfortable moment occurs, do not apologize for being onto them; just continue to trust your instincts, keep your eyes open, and remain vigilant about noticing any future inconsistencies.

Recently, a good friend of mine had been struggling to get past some tough times in her life. She had finally figured out that her poor decisions and life choices were not only unproductive in helping her achieve success, but they were impeding it. In order to grow past that negative period in her life, she realized she needed to reach out to a group of her so-called friends to request some time and space to gather her thoughts in solitude.

Instead of these so-called friends offering their support and understanding as she worked on improving her life, they showed their true colors and actually became irate and dismissive with her; because she changed her mind about how she had been leading her life...the spiraling-out-of-control-life that these "friends" had been gleefully cheering her in leading only because it fulfilled *their* needs, not hers.

TIP 12 | DISMISSIVE OF YOUR NEEDS

Does this "misery loves company" story sound familiar? If so, do you have any of these so-called friends that you may need to confront or leave behind?

The final "emotional parasite" characteristic is their failure to apologize when confronted. Emotional parasites are noted for blaming others while taking no personal responsibility for being their normal "victim" selves. Unfortunately this personality type is so common, that we have all come across this red flag behavior when dealing with these types of people.

Have you ever noticed when you call someone out on saying or doing something you didn't like, rather than receiving an apology from that person, you receive a defensive response? Instead of simply owning (taking responsibility for) and acknowledging how his or her words or actions negatively affected you, they actually express unfounded anger toward you in their defensiveness for being called out on their own crap.

TIP 13 | GETTING DEFENSIVE?

Whereas, in a healthy relationship, when one unintentionally says or does something that upsets or hurts the other person, the respectful response is to gain an understanding of their perspective and to offer them a sincere apology (while putting aside any discomfort one may feel by being "confronted").

To help you become more comfortable in handling confrontational situations, take a moment to figure out some different scenarios where healthy boundaries might be challenged and list them below. Follow each scenario with how you would ideally resolve these conflicts:

1 _____

_____

2 _____

_____

3 _____

_____

4 _____

_____

When it comes to healthy personal relationships, the biggest mistake I see too many people making is when they inaccurately label "acquaintances" as "friends."

The problem is, too many people have been falsely programmed, from an early age, to just accept other people at face value and label them a "friend" while they likely don't even have a clear definition of what that term really means.

For most, there is no clear logic as to why someone befriends another other than the fact that they have had some positive "emotional" reaction to the other person when they initially met. And because they apparently "like" each other, it must mean that they are "friends." But isn't it also true that we like acquaintances we meet? So does that therefore mean we should immediately label that "acquaintance," a "friend" due to that initially positive emotional response?

TIP 14 | FRIEND OR ACQUAINTANCE?

After helping several of my students, clients, and friends differentiate between considering a person an acquaintance versus a friend, I concluded there are six "universal" adjectives that best describe a healthy and happy personal relationship.

1. *Safe* — How safe do you feel speaking openly with this person? Can you share intimate and personal things about your life with this person without worrying about them using the information against you?

2. *Reliable* — How reliable is this person to you? Can you rely on them to be there for you or follow up on your behalf? Have they been there for you in the past? Do they do what they say they'll do?

3. *Trustworthy* — How trustworthy is this person to you? Are they truly being honest with you or do you feel they are just manipulating you in some way to gain your trust for their own purposes?

4. *Supportive* — Is this person supportive of your goals, dreams, and passions? Do they cheer you on in your efforts and give you their true support, or do you sense they have their own hidden agenda for why they interact with you? Do you let them sabotage your success by allowing them to project their fears and insecurities onto you? Are they truly in your court? Do they have your best interest at heart, or their own?

5. *Myself (they let me be me)* — Does this person let you be yourself around them? Do you feel like you morph into somebody else or that you can truly be yourself whenever you are around them? Do they try to change you because they actually want you to be someone else while claiming the "improvement" is for your own good?

6. *Don't Guilt* — Does this person ever make you feel guilty for not wanting to go along with what *they* want to do? Do you feel like you are compromising yourself to be friends with them?

Notice that the six universal adjectives all require actions/their commitment and are not simply words (i.e., Don't tell me, *Show* me!).

Take some time to evaluate the people around you (especially your closest friends) and ask yourself:

- Are they being authentic with their intentions?

- Is their personality consistent among different people and situations?

Take a few moments and go through the following shortened version of my "Friends Exercise" then ask yourself:

"ARE THEY FRIENDS OR JUST ACQUAINTANCES?"

Write down the top six adjectives that you believe best describes a "friend." In the following boxes, rate their level of possessing that quality from 1 - 5 (1-poor, 2-fair, 3-average 4-good, 5-outstanding). Ideally, they should possess at least 3 or higher in at least four of the six adjective descriptions.

Friend's Name	Adjective 1.	Adjective 2.	Adjective 3.	Adjective 4.	Adjective 5.	Adjective 6.
	Loyal	Supportive	Driven	Creative	Honest	Funny
Example: DARLA	3	4	2	4	5	5

Now, using the chart below, re-rank your same friends (from above). This time, apply the following revised *universal* qualities. Once you see your results, they should help you differentiate between people you are mistakenly considering true "friends," versus the "acquaintances" they actually are.

Friend's Name	Adjective 1.	Adjective 2.	Adjective 3.	Adjective 4.	Adjective 5.	Adjective 6.
	Safe	Reliable	Trustworthy	Supportive	Myself	Don't Guilt

ACT THE WAY YOU'D LIKE TO BE AND SOON YOU'LL BE THE WAY YOU ACT.

~ BOB DYLAN

Be Distinct
Or Be Extinct

{Tips 15 – 19}

IT IS ALWAYS YOUR NEXT MOVE.

~ NAPOLEON HILL

BE DISTINCT OR BE EXTINCT

MANY YEARS AGO, I was at a conference when I heard motivational speaker and business coach, Tom Peters, utter these five important words: "Be Distinct, Or Be Extinct."

To grow and achieve your long-term success, it is crucial that you always find ways to distinguish yourself from others.

Most people "go with the flow" and never challenge the status quo. This approach is fine for someone who is content to live an average life. But if you are someone who really wants to experience a higher level of success, then you will need to be very clear about your intentions.

Successful people don't coast through life. They break out of the box and make things happen! To really be distinct and stand out amongst your fellow classmates, you need to sit down and decide on:

- What, specifically, you want to pursue in your personal and professional life

- Visualizing what that success will look like

- Creating short-term and long-term goals for achieving your success

- <u>Taking Action</u> on your goals

Most people fail to achieve their success because they never take action on their goals, remain stagnant, and eventually...they become extinct.

Amongst the many attributes successful people possess, a trait they consistently share is that they establish their own signature brand. By studying successful people that you'd like to emulate, you will get some concrete ideas about to how to enhance and evolve your own signature brand.

Naturally, your style will morph over time as you grow and change. But just as we all have our own unique finger prints, voice signatures, etc., your honed personal brand will always remain exclusive to you and one that you will present to the world to help you stand out in the crowd.

Whether you're a college freshman or are in your final year, you're going to want to start creating your own personal brand right away. It's never too early to start considering your decisions regarding those questions. How *do* you want to present yourself to the world?

With the Internet and media in general, it's next to impossible not to be inundated with countless looks with which to experiment. This is where your answers to those questions will help you in molding your signature image so others will quickly identify and remember you by (think: Justin Timberlake, Zooey Deschanel, Lady Gaga [well, only Lady Gaga if you *want* to come off as an ultra zany performance artist]). Whatever approach you decide to take, distinguish yourself from others by being unique and memorable.

TIP 15 | ESTABLISH YOUR OWN PERSONAL BRAND

In addition to your appearance affecting how others might perceive you, obviously it's your scintillating personality that will truly round out your own personal brand.

Some people project cool or laid back, while others may be perceived as uptight or intense...however you evolve your personal brand, my suggestion would be to embrace it and own it!

Embrace your personality quirks...If you are a geek, then be an <u>Awesome Geek</u>! Otherwise, you won't come off to others as unique and genuine. And don't forget, there are a lot of cool, successful geeks out there (e.g., Bill Gates, Larry M. Jacobson, Mark Zuckerberg, pretty much anyone who attends Comic-Con, etc., etc., etc.)!

Jot down some ideas as to how you would like to hone your personal brand to catapult you into a stand out amongst the crowd:

1 _____

_____

2 _____

_____

3 _____

_____

As a young adult preparing for the "real world," you're required to have more than just book smarts. Making your way toward achieving your success requires you to learn to listen to your instincts and learn how use and follow good common sense.

Your intuition is that little voice inside your head, or that uncomfortable feeling in your gut, which helps you differentiate whether something *feels* right versus "off" or wrong — even if it doesn't quite seem logical at the time. As for having good common sense... sadly, it's not as common as you'd think. So utilize that to your advantage to stand out by using good common sense!

TIP 16 | TRUST YOUR OWN INSTINCTS

Unfortunately, many young adults have been programmed, since their formative years, to simply override their instincts by being constantly reminded to "keep their heads down," "look the other way," "don't make waves," "let someone else handle things," "don't challenge authority," etc., etc., etc.

Consequently, many have learned to tune themselves out, and therefore, haven't learned to listen to, follow, or trust their own instincts. Instead, they often just ignore their inner voices and overthink themselves into paralysis. Or they just make excuses and allow themselves to have a knee-jerk reaction only to then second-guess themselves and their decisions.

NOW is the time to WAKE UP YOUR INNER VOICE and listen to what your instincts are telling you! Your instincts are actually the foundation for your own empowerment. Don't allow yourself to get swayed by negative or unsupportive comments made by others. Don't allow other people to "get inside your head" causing you to overthink, or even worse, react out of incorrectly forecasting how you think they might respond to your decisions or ideas.

Successful people "go for it." They check their fears at the door. To positively impact your desired expectations and *probable* (versus possible) outcomes for success, trust your instincts by:

- Spotting opportunities

- Reaffirm your intentions which will be motivational and self-empowering

- Take whatever action steps are necessary to achieve your goals

If you are like the majority of today's college students, then you are probably posting away about some intimate aspects of your life on various social media sites (Instagram, Pinterest, Twitter, Facebook, etc.) — most likely without even thinking twice about what these postings might be saying about you.

It is extremely important to always keep in mind that whenever you meet someone new (or even when you are simply leaving your home), you are putting your personal brand on display because it is how you (either consciously or unconsciously) want others to perceive, identify, and remember you by.

TIP 17 | THE REALITY OF SOCIAL MEDIA

This advice especially holds true for social media sites. Your postings serve as portals to your personal life *and* your brand, leaving you exposed for others to observe (and judge) you from the comfort of their own computer screens. And if you think there is no harm posting crazy, irresponsible pictures, verbal rants, etc. because you are "young and there will be no real repercussions..." think again!

Like Las Vegas, what happens on the 'net stays on the 'net. Sure, it may seem obvious, but you really need to be careful and aware of every single thing you post on social media sites. Because once you post them, despite any future efforts to delete them, they will <u>very</u> likely continue to be accessible to others (including future bosses and in-laws) for-ev-er!

As a general rule, I strongly suggest that you only choose to post things on your social media sites that truly support or represent your personal brand. Like your unique look and personality, your postings should intrigue — not offend — potential followers, or more importantly, potential employers.

<u>Your pictures and written posts</u> should positively reinforce your brand, and describe how you would like others to perceive you. YOU are in control of what that perception could be.

What I would like you to keep in mind, is that successful people utilize social media to help them share their personal vision and goals by explaining to their friends/followers/connections how they plan to help other people by doing...(fill in the blank).

Just as in the virtual world, there's nothing that can destroy a personal brand or make a worst first — or *lasting* — impression like having bad manners (i.e., poor social etiquette) can.

You always want to make sure that you behave appropriately in the various social and/or professional situations and settings that you attend. Make sure that you do not inadvertently offend or embarrass yourself or your hosts.

If you find yourself in a new or unknown social or professional situation, research the proper social etiquette for that occasion or event ahead of time. Or speak to someone who has had experience **TIP 18** | GOOD SOCIAL ETIQUETTE (MIND YOUR MANNERS) with those types of events so that you can always put your best "you" forward.

Don't overlook researching the expected attire for your event — dress appropriately. There is a big difference between casual, business casual, cocktail, and a dressy (black-tie) affair.

Your goal should always be to make a positive first impression. It was Shakespeare who said, "All the world's a stage…" So call it what you will — costume, wardrobe, outfit, attire...

Just remember to "dress the part!"

And all those niceties your parents hopefully taught you when you were growing up…"say please," "thank you," and "excuse me..." Yes, they were solid lessons and are very much, still important.

As a matter of fact, I strongly hold the belief that guys should always offer to hold a door open for others. This courteous gesture should not, by any means, be considered as anti-feminist. It's called, "being a gentleman." And it is important to be so at all times. If you find yourself wincing right now. Don't. You can <u>never</u> go wrong by honoring good old-fashioned, time-tested manners.

Finally, pay attention to your eating habits: Do not talk with your mouth full, no elbows on the table, place your napkin on your lap, etc.

Others may not always acknowledge or recognize your good etiquette and manners, but they sure will remember your poor ones.

As with your physical appearance and manner-isms, ultimately how you verbally communicate with others will also play a major role in your overall personal branding.

It is essential that you acquire exemplary written and verbal skills before you graduate from college so that you can effectively communicate with others in the workplace and elsewhere. If you do not feel comfortable speaking in front of larger groups of people, then I highly recommend that you consider joining a social networking group such as Toastmasters International, or some other college or profession-ally sponsored program or organiza-tion that can assist you with public speaking.

TIP 19 | LEARN HOW TO COMMUNICATE EFFECTIVELY WITH OTHERS

As for honing your writing abilities, I have found that there are two tools that every college student should habitually utilize in order to help them be-come more successful: a dictionary and a thesaurus. While that suggestion may seem plainly obvious, and everyone seems to be well-aware of their existence, they forget to actually utilize them!

If you ever find yourself unsure of a particular word, there is no shame in looking it up ("A word looked up is a word remembered"). You should always acquaint yourself with words that you don't understand or aren't sure how to use. You never want to use a word incorrectly or in the wrong context when writing or speaking to others, as it may tarnish your credibility and personal brand.

Also, *always* proofread your written work — college papers, emails, etc. before you submit them. Run spell check, catch typos, and confirm that you have accurately and effectively used all of your fancy vocabulary words correctly so that you properly convey your intended message.

Similarly, while I'm mentioning vocabulary words, I am compelled to remind you to use a thesaurus to *galvanize* you into finding new ways to say the same old thing. Nothing tends to bore and/or turn off readers more than when writers continuously use the same words over and over and over again. (I hope I'm not being ironic as I write this portion of TIP 19!)

Stay creative!

Time Management: Successful Study Secrets and Tips

{Tips 20 – 22}

TIME MANAGEMENT:

THE SECRET OF GETTING AHEAD IS GETTING STARTED. THE SECRET OF GETTING STARTED IS BREAKING YOUR COMPLEX OVERWHELMING TASKS INTO MANAGEABLE TASKS, AND THEN STARTING ON THE FIRST ONE.

~ MARK TWAIN

SO, HOW DO you find the time to strike up a good balance between managing your time to effectively study, while also enjoying a busy social life? First and foremost, you need to be <u>brutally honest</u> with yourself about the type of college student you really are.

Ask yourself:

"Do I study hard, or
do I hardly study?"

If you answered "hardly study," then it's time for a reality check. Are you really surprised by the low grades that you are likely receiving? And if that's the case — that you are doing poorly in school — I'm sure you do not like the way it feels. Failing to live up to one's true potential naturally takes a serious toll on one's self-esteem.

Speaking from firsthand experience back when I wasn't living up to my potential and used excuses like, "It's too hard," or "I'm not as smart as the other kids in my classes," my past excuses which "justified" my poor study habits only harmed my own future.

If you're not reaping the rewards from living up to your true potential, it's not because you are any less intelligent than your classmates.

Harsh truth:

You are just lazier, more fearful,
and less disciplined than they are.

Don't fool yourself by coming up with lame excuses like I did before I got my act together.

Know this:

1. You are not fooling anyone but yourself (your parents and professors aren't buying it either).

2. As the cliché goes, you're only cheating yourself (clichés are clichés because of their universal truths!).

Everything you are doing TODAY is paving the way in determining how great and successful your life can be. Trust me, the earlier you make the conscious decision to apply yourself in <u>all</u> your actions, and make sound strategic decisions, the better off your future will be.

Here's a HUGE "bang for the buck" tip:

What if I told you that by simply applying better time management skills to your current study habits, you would not only improve your study time (which would lead to better grades), but you would also have more time to socialize or do whatever you wanted?

What if I also told you that I could show you easier ways to study so that you would no longer have to stay up late or pull all-nighters to finish your homework and/or reading assignments?

What if I could teach you how to use your time more wisely so you could really understand and rem-

TIP 20 | CREATING EFFECTIVE STUDYING PLANS

ember the material you were learning and have better recall of the material for your tests and during class time?

Ready?

Creating Effective Study Plans:

At the beginning of each new semester, sit down with all your new class syllabuses and break down all future quizzes and test dates, as well as all future due dates for your reading and project assignments — creating lists for each course you're taking.

Then on a weekly basis, map out all of your reading and homework assignments that are due for that particular week, breaking down when you plan to read and/or outline your assignments.

For example, if you have a 100-page reading assignment for that upcoming week, divide reading those 100 pages into more manageable pieces ($100 \div 7 = 15$ or so pages). So instead of stressing, trying to cram and retain 100 pages of information over one or two days, by breaking the reading assignment down into smaller increments, over the seven day period, you will now only have to read those 14+ pages each day.

This simple technique really will help you improve managing your study time by effectively allowing you to read all the pages by the required due dates, as well as enabling you to retain the info (beyond just "regurgitating" it on test day).

In addition to creating effective study plans, allowing ample time to prepare yourself for upcoming quizzes and exams is vital to your academic success.

Remember I mentioned I have firsthand experience messing up? Well when I got to college, I finally figured out that if I didn't improve my study habits, I was simply not going to succeed.

As far as all-nighters go, wasting precious time you can never get back without ever achieving the results you desire is ludicrous. Why wait until the last minute to try and cram in all that (costly!) information for one horrendous night of exhaustive studying, overwhelming yourself and impeding your true potential???

TIP 21 | AVOIDING THE DREADED ALL-NIGHTER

I learned this tip the hard way. But committing to improving my study habits brought my C grades up to A's. So I strongly recommend that you outline and begin studying your class notes, professors' lectures, and assignments several days before the upcoming quiz or exam.

Like I suggested you do with your homework and reading assignments, break down your study notes over a predetermined amount of days leading up to your quiz or exam.

For example, if you have 20 pages of class/professor's notes to study or memorize, if you start studying five days before the quiz or exam, you would only have to study or memorize four manageable pages of notes per day.

When I was in college, I would start each new study session by first reviewing the notes/study pages from the prior day before I started studying the new notes. The consistent reviewing and repetition really helped to reinforce the material that I had already studied. I felt that I had learned all of the material, and I was fully prepared for the quiz or exam.

By avoiding the dreaded all-nighter, I could retain the subject matter much better than if I had tortured myself by trying to cram/study it all the night before. I cannot express to you how great it felt to truly be prepared and to live up to my potential.

Another study technique that I acquired during my college years was a little game that I liked to call, "Thinking like the Professor."

During my class lectures, I tried to always pay extra close attention to any material that I felt the professor was really focusing on during their lectures. If there was ever a time where I was unclear about the subject matter/material, I would try to schedule an appointment to meet with the professor outside of the classroom to get further clarification.

Once I had his or her undivided attention, I would ask the professor what material they suggested I really focus on that would be most useful for preparing for the upcoming quiz and exam.

TIP 22 | THINKING LIKE THE PROFESSOR

I also used to ask my professors if they could provide me with any examples of papers or practice exams that I could review in order to give me a better understanding of what they expected from us on the upcoming quiz or exam.

I always tried to be extremely respectful of their time, but I also never overlooked an opportunity to stand out among my fellow classmates and make a good first impression.

In fact, because of the positive impressions I made on some of my previous professors, and the relationships that I forged with them outside of the classroom (i.e., during our scheduled meetings, extracurricular activities, etc.), I gained their ongoing respect and trust.

To this day, I still maintain professional (and some, personal) relationships with several of my college and graduate school professors. This bond has resulted in their providing me with professional recommendations, references, and even opened the door to speaking engagements.

I cannot stress this enough: the sooner you start using your time wisely and dedicating yourself to growing your own success, the better off your entire life will be. It really does go by quickly. Always make your precious time count — it's the only commodity you can never get back.

Your future self will thank you.

From the Classroom to the Boardroom

{Tips 23 – 25}

SUCCESSFUL AND UNSUCCESSFUL PEOPLE DO NOT VARY GREATLY IN THEIR ABILITIES. THEY VARY IN THEIR DESIRES TO REACH THEIR POTENTIAL.

~ JOHN MAXWELL

MOST AMERICANS NEVER learn how to "work smart" because they are usually spinning their wheels working too hard. Are your parents or any of your college classmates workaholics?

If so, I can relate. I used to work way too hard in the workplace until one of my Pepperdine University Business School professors taught me a great secret to managing not only my workload and productivity, but my boss as well.

The studying/planning techniques and habits I had established back in college served me well in terms of managing my time, but I had yet to learn the art of managing...The Boss. Or more specifically, managing my boss's expectations — a key strategy in achieving success in the workplace.

After you graduate, you can apply the same time management study skills you utilized in college to all of your future professional endeavors. And just as those good habits will have created more time for socializing in college, the tips in this section will help you create more time to cultivate your social life outside of work — not always an easy task with seemingly nonstop work demands.

Also, the more you focus your attention on improving your time management skills in the workplace, the more aware and agile you will become in handling any unexpected problems/opportunities as they arise.

This is an incredibly important skill to possess — to not only know how to be nimble under duress, but to have created the extra cushion of time to be able to handle those unexpected matters in real time.

Successful people tend to be highly focused and organized. The more time you dedicate toward learning good time management early on, the more you will be able to always take advantage of future opportunities.

Whenever your boss or your clients give you work projects or assignments, like in college, sit down on a weekly basis and review and prioritize all your current job projects. This may sound really simple, but you would be surprised by just how many people never do this simple task in their professional lives — just like college, many of them simply neglect to plan ahead.

As I suggested regarding your college homework assignments, familiarize yourself with, and prioritize, all future work deadlines for your upcoming week's demands (meetings, contacts, etc.). Do this each and every week. By doing so, you will be breaking down your weekly work assignments and projects into manageable daily tasks.

TIP 23 | PLAN FOR THE WORK WEEK AHEAD

At the end of your work day, or right when you arrive in the morning, pause to write down (old-school style with pen to paper) all of the things that you wish to accomplish — be as specific as possible. Your daily list should include: tending to phone calls, emails, meetings, project deliverables (if any are due that day), etc. As you complete each item, check or cross them off your daily list of things to do.

This is a great way to not only keep yourself on task, but it will also provide you with a great feeling of accomplishment when you review your overall progress at the end of each day.

Remember, a typical work day is only eight hours long. Try to make sure that your daily tasks are realistic enough to be able to complete within the time frame you've allocated. By doing so, you'll be setting yourself up to successfully achieve what you've set out to accomplish. And you do not want to find yourself falling behind or feeling frustrated and defeated. The more aware you are of your deadlines and progress, the more successful and reliable you will become to your boss, clients, and yourself.

Avoid overcommitting yourself in order to try to impress your boss or clients. The goal is to learn how to work smarter, not harder.

Overcommitting or overpromising to others in the workplace is like trying to cram for a college all-nighter. You may not achieve your desired outcome or best work, or even worse, you may find yourself continuously making excuses for what went wrong. There is an old saying in business, "Under-promise and Over-deliver." This is a great approach to working smart that will leave your boss and clients pleasantly surprised when they get more than what they initially expected. You will be doing yourself a huge favor learning how to incorporate good time management skills into your professional life.

TIP 24 | MANAGING YOUR BOSS AND CLIENTS

To help you prevent yourself from overcommitting your time and energy at work, I will now share that secret I learned from Pepperdine MBA Professor, Richard Riordan regarding managing the expectations of your boss and clients in order to make your project workload more manageable.

Presuming you can effectively only manage five projects at one time (and you are also unable to delegate any of that workload to your co-workers), my professor's advice was to solicit your boss's and clients' advice to help you prioritize scheduling your current workload. He then suggested taking it a step further by finding out if either your boss or client(s) want you to take on any additional or new work. And if so, "how would they prefer that you prioritize the extra responsibilities?"

The goal is to consult with your boss and/or client(s) to come together in deciding on which of your current five projects should either be delayed or removed in order to incorporate any additional responsibilities/priorities or new projects into your already impacted workload.

Essentially, you will be managing your boss's and clients' expectations by including them in your various workload decisions in order to ensure that you always meet your mutually anticipated deadlines.

I have been spreading my message that success is really all about never being afraid to ask "why?" I strongly believe that in order to become really good at something, you not only need to learn "how" something is done, but more importantly, "why."

We were all born with the instinct to question. Think about it...most toddlers innocently annoy their parents by repeatedly asking them, "why? Why? WHY?" However, by the time these same inquisitive children enter their formative teenage years, they have all but lost their desire to ask "why?"

Why?

TIP 25 | ALWAYS EMBRACE THE "WHY"

Because nowadays most people simply live life in a world of "how?" "Just tell me how I can I get that job," or "How do I make all that money?" or "Just tell me *how*, and I will just do it!"...No questions asked.

There is no creativity in only wanting to know, "how?" It really is just the poster-word for accepting the status quo...merely accepting answers at face value instead of digging deeper by asking, and understanding, WHY. Truly successful people seem to consistently go that extra mile to figure out the answers to "why?"

It really is so unfortunate that most people have simply become too afraid to question others. Theoretical (non-practical) thinking allows one to understand not only "how" something is done, but "why" it is so. By understanding the "why," successful outcomes are much likelier to be recreated on a consistent basis. Asking "why?" facilitates creative problem-solving and fosters improvement upon the status quo.

I believe that successful people choose to embrace the "why" because it provides them with overwhelming advantages; it helps them figure out new ways to improve upon old ideas and continue to innovate based upon changing times. But most importantly, it provides them with the confidence to discontinue processes or systems that no longer work, in order to create new and improved strategies to ultimately beat out their competition.

Dreams are for Bedtime, Goals are for Success!

{Tips 26 – 28}

DREAMS
are for
BEDTIME,

> THE GREATER PART OF
> ALL THE MISCHIEF IN THE
> WORLD ARISES FROM
> THE FACT THAT MEN
> DO NOT SUFFICIENTLY
> UNDERSTAND THEIR
> OWN AIMS.
>
> ~ GOETHE

GOALS
are

SUCCESS!
FOR

THE MOST IMPORTANT step toward achieving your goals is to *take action*!

Unfortunately, many people tend to confuse their dreams for their goals. For example, many people believe that "being rich" is a goal. Well...it's actually not. It is just a dream because the statement, "I want to be rich" is not *specific* enough to be considered a goal.

There is nothing in that five-word statement that would motivate anyone to take immediate action — it is too vague. "I want to be rich" does not specify any clear dollar amount or time frame, and therefore makes it harder to create or assign any specific action steps to achieve that <u>dream</u>.

Whereas, stating, "I want to be earning $100,000 a year by the time I am 25 years old," establishes personal accountability.

Why?

Because by stating the $100,000, it *specifies* a clear dollar amount to be earned within a *specific* period of time...by 25. Because there is such *specificity* in the statement, *specific* actions would need to be considered and pursued in order to achieve the <u>goal</u> by the predetermined period of time.

The statement itself is a call to action. In order to achieve it, planning would be necessary. Some example questions to research would be:

- What type of education would be needed?

- What type of job or internship would increase skills?

- What kind of extracurricular activities/experiences would enhance the *probability* of achieving this goal?

So as you begin to manifest what you truly want to accomplish in your life, always remember to be *specific*: dreams are bedtime, goals are for success!

Fear, not one's lack of abilities, is the greatest reason why most people often fail to achieve the success they desire. Most people simply cannot get out of their own way.

Why fear? Because the majority of people either lack the necessary information, or the awareness to succeed. They instead succumb to their fears and never make any real efforts to ever get out of their own negative comfort zones. To do so would involve doing the necessary work to improve their current situations, or even better, understand how to avoid them altogether.

TIP 26 | GET OUT OF YOUR OWN WAY

To quote the great Zig Ziglar, "You don't have to be great to start, but you have to be start to be great."

For better or worse, early life experiences (influences from parents, teachers, friends, etc.) impact how one reacts to their fears and negative emotions — whether one succumbs to, or overcomes, their fears. Most well-established successful adults overcame debilitating self-sabotaging obstacles by choosing to shift their unhealthy attitudes and learned perspectives as they began manifesting their desired outcomes.

To help you overcome your self-sabotaging fears, this outline of my "Transformational Model for Getting Out of Your Own Way" will guide you through the tough process of change to get to that light at the end of the tunnel:

1. **The Awakening Phase (The Realization Phase)** — Ask yourself, "SO, HOW'S THAT WORKING FOR YOU?" It is a simple question that really only requires you to be honest with yourself and address those things in your life that are no longer working/supporting your desired outcomes for success. Commit to taking complete ownership of your life, and stop blaming others for your own bad decisions, choices, and actions. Begin empowering yourself and stop projecting your own negative programming and feelings onto yourself and others.

2. **The Tunnel of Transition Phase (The Uncomfortable phase)** — Just like traveling through a real tunnel, this phase can at times feel almost claustrophobic. The darkness and uncertainty one experiences during any unknown transition in life usually causes one to feel uncomfortable and overwhelmed. Override your feelings of anxiety while staying focused on embracing your future, healthier self. Just

remember to breathe. Don't panic. Remind yourself that you have chosen this new path for a reason: Your old life wasn't working for you anymore.

3. **The Transformation Phase (The Paradigm Shift)** — That empowering moment in your life when you get to experience the success that you desire. To reach this final phase of awareness, you will need to be persistent as you manage your fears and uncertainty so you can reach the light at the end of your tunnel.

Not only will you need to have cleared your tunnel of transition, but you will also need to continuously re-evaluate your ongoing goals and objectives so that you allow yourself to remain your transformed and best self.

Write down how you plan to transition out of a current negative comfort zone to get out of your own way, and onto finding your best self:

1 |
_____

_____

2 |
_____

To get started on your path to success, I have created the following list to help you organize your action steps to achieve your goals:

1. **What is your true passion or desire?** — What is the one thing that continuously drives you to pursue your passion/desires? What makes you want to leap out of bed in the morning? What are you compelled to tell the world that you believe will benefit all who will listen?

2. **Create goals that will lead you to live the** life you desire (e.g., your passion) — Remember, dreams are for bedtime, *goals* are for success! Goals require *specific* actions be taken within a predetermined period of time in order to achieve those goals.

TIP 27 | *"P.P.I.E."* CHECKLIST FOR ORGANIZING YOUR SUCCESS

3. **Clearly define your vision and purpose (e.g., mission)** — Be very clear about what you want to achieve when you define your vision and purpose. Make sure that your vision and purpose align with your passions and goals. It is extremely important that you are able to clearly communicate your goals so that other people will be able to quickly understand and identify with your stated cause or goals.

4. **Evaluate and implement your specific, realistic action steps** — To ensure that your action plan continues to best align with your passions and goals, be very clear about your decisions regarding the three elements to the right:

- **TIME**
  ...amount of hours dedicated toward achieving your goals

- **MONEY**
  ...cost of investing in your goals

- **PEOPLE**
  ...with whom you choose to associate and/or reach out to in order to accomplish your goals

It is very important that you maintain your awareness regarding these considerations as they will have a direct impact on either positively or negatively affecting your outcome.

Equally important, make sure that you take the time to properly evaluate and adjust your action plan whenever necessary to ensure that you continuously achieve the results you desire.

P.P.I.E.:
Prioritize your goals
Plan your actions
Implement your plans
Evaluate your actions and desired outcomes

Too many adults have developed a phobia of making mistakes or have simply chosen to conform to the status quo. The irony is that the biggest mistake parents, teachers, and society have made has been not teaching youth that it's actually not only okay, but a growth opportunity to make mistakes! I think I've made it pretty clear by now, I have made my fair share. And I did learn from them. But there are some things I could have avoided suffering through had I had the foresight to avoid the following seven traps:

1. **Thinking you are the smartest person in the room** — Despite what your parents, friends, significant other, or reflection in the mirror tells you...you are not the smartest person in the room. There is never a positive return on being a "know it all." Listen more, talk less. You may actually learn from others if you give them an opportunity to speak.

2. **Not getting out of your own way** — One of the main reasons why so many people never seem to achieve their goals and success is because they simply succumb to their fears and insecurities. They never make any real efforts to get out of their own negative comfort zone. Remember, success and failure are both the result of intentional decisions.

3. **Always looking for the other shoe to drop** — Stop expecting the worst, stop assuming the worst, and stop looking for things to go wrong. Start trusting yourself, the process, and others. A good rule to remember, "Where there is no smoke, there is no fire."

4. **It's my way or the highway** — If you are someone who must always see or do things your way, your own rigid behavior may create unnecessary barriers, preventing you from achieving your success. Most people don't become successful on their own. Everyone needs help from somebody at some point in their life.

5. **Don't play the victim** — Stop feeling sorry for yourself because of something that was "done to you." YOU are in control of your own emotional outcomes. You are the one in charge of how you will react to the events in your life. So the only person that has control over your life is YOU. If you choose to give up that power to someone else, ultimately that's your decision. Therefore it can be your decision to take back your power. If you want to change things in your life, then start taking responsibility for your own actions and stop blaming others for your own poor decisions.

6. **Keeping up with the Joneses** — "There is only one you, everyone else is taken!" Do not succumb to the urge to compare yourself to others. Do not allow negative comments or views of a select few dictate how you think everyone perceives you. You only have control over how you decide to "package yourself" with your chosen personal brand. How others perceive you from that point on is out of your control. Just focus on following your own path and staying true to your own unique and authentic self. If you stay on that course, your confidence and special attributes will shine through.

7. **Getting stuck in your own head** — Negative thoughts can turn you into your own worst enemy. It really is counterproductive to achieving your success when you are overly concerned about your physical appearance, the material trappings you own, and worrying about how other people are going to perceive your ideas and/or actions. Don't drive yourself crazy by overanalyzing every little detail or decision to the point where you become too paralyzed to take any action. Trust that your knowledge, instincts, abilities, and competence is what will lead you to achieving your success. Trust yourself.

The Art of the Pause: Making Good Strategic Decisions
{Tips 29 – 34}

THE ART OF
THE PAUSE

> LOOK FOR YOUR CHOICES,
> PICK THE BEST ONE, AND
> THEN GO WITH IT.
>
> ~ PAT RILEY

MAKING GOOD STRATEGIC DECISIONS

BECAUSE SO MANY college students spend the majority of their time responding to their fears, low self-esteem, and the chaos that surrounds them in their young adult lives, they often tend to make quick, emotionally-driven, and unproductive choices. They do so based solely on reactions derived from their own negative emotional programming, as opposed to learning, from an early age, how to remain calm, and make strategic and logical decisions that will often benefit, or resolve their ultimate outcomes.

Like an anchor that holds a ship steady in unchartered waters, whenever faced with an uncomfortable decision, take a moment to step back and pause so you can focus and weigh all your strategic alternatives and options (despite whatever appears to be going on around you). As opposed to making quick, emotionally-driven decisions that will most often derail you.

To help you begin differentiating between strategic, versus emotional, decisions during one of the most critical and emotionally-driven times in your life, I am going to introduce you to several decision-making strategies that will help you to improve your *probable* outcomes for success.

Once you become clear on the difference, you will start thinking more strategically and less emotionally. You will start executing more strategically-driven decisions that will help you to become better aligned with your goals and you will make decisions that will help you to consistently optimize your *probable* outcomes for success.

PROBABILITY implies decisiveness
(That WILL probably happen)
POSSIBILITY implies uncertainty
(That COULD possibly happen)

The next time you are faced with a difficult decision (big or small), I would like you to ask yourself the following question:

"WHAT IS THE *PROBABILITY* THAT MY DECISION WILL LEAD TO A SUCCESSFUL OUTCOME, AND HOW WILL THIS DECISION GET ME ANY CLOSER TO ACHIEVING MY OVERALL GOALS?"

TIP 29 | PROBABLE, VERSUS POSSIBLE, OUTCOMES FOR SUCCESS

Many insecure and emotionally-driven people often make rash decisions that lead to, at best, possible (instead of *probable*) outcomes for success. Whereas, successful and secure people avoid wasting any of their precious time, resources, or energy making anything but strategic decisions that most often lead to *probable* outcomes for success.

To help you begin thinking more strategically, I would like you to ask yourself the following question before you make any future decisions:

"What is the *probability,* versus the possibility, that my future decision will be a good strategic use of my time, resources, and energy and how will this decision help me to achieve my short-term or long-term goals for success?"

Rather than trying to convince yourself, or simply please someone else by making yet another emotionally-driven decision that may derail your future plans, take a moment to <u>pause</u> and ask yourself if this pending decision is coming from your strategic head, or your emotional heart. And then figure out how the outcome of this decision may ultimately benefit or hurt you personally, professionally, etc.

So many college students become so conditioned by the media, advertisers, and so-called professionals that if they don't immediately jump or take advantage of some new craze, idea, or opportunity in that exact moment, then it may be lost forever.

Advertisers pay big money to marketers to subliminally (or sometimes overtly) manipulate your better judgment by telling you what you appear to be lacking in your life, or even worse, what you can't *possibly* live without.

You are the only one who truly knows or understands how your decisions (*probable* vs. possible outcomes) can play out in the bigger

TIP 30 | JUST SLEEP ON IT!

picture of your future success. So step back and give yourself any extra time you may need to be able to answer how your decision may ultimately benefit you in the future...as opposed to benefiting the person on the other end who may be pressuring you to "close the deal."

Bottom line:

If you are not sure how this particular "must have" item or scenario will immediately benefit your future *probable* outcomes for success, then I highly suggest that you JUST SLEEP ON IT and keep the following tips in mind:

1. Do not rush yourself into immediately deciding on anything.

2. Do not talk yourself into making any emotionally-driven decisions before you do your research and determine all the outcomes and facts.

3. Do not fall prey to anyone's manipulation (e.g., pushiness) — you have every right to demand your boundaries be respected.

4. Do not allow yourself to feel manipulated into making any decisions that you may later regret.

5. Always keep the old adage in mind, "If it sounds too good to be true, then it probably is."

You would not believe how many people neglect taking the time to plan ahead to address how to properly handle important opportunities, events, or decisions before they actually occur.

For example, after you graduate college, you tell yourself you will take a part-time/full-time job for only a year until you get on your feet professionally and/or financially, only to find yourself years later still working in this same unfulfilling, dead-end job with no foreseeable exit plan in the future.

Successful college graduates need to learn, from an early age, how to strategically conserve their personal/financial resources so they do not

TIP 31 | CONSERVING YOUR RESOURCES

find themselves working hard, instead of smart...foolishly spinning their wheels, falling deeper into a hole as they exhaust their time, energy, and/or money.

Before you decide to commit your valuable resources, always ask yourself, "How much time, energy, and/or money will my decision ultimately cost me — personally and financially?"

Never make any important personal, professional, or financial decisions in your life without first weighing all the pros and cons.

Prior to acting upon your strategically-driven (versus emotionally-driven) decisions, I highly suggest that you do all of your homework and research ahead of time by calculating and determining just how long it may take you to recoup or benefit from all of the time, energy, and/or money you may have to invest before you see any returns/reward resulting from executing your decision(s).

When referring to intentions, I am describing the purpose, or catalyst, that is ultimately driving one's decisions. When it comes to emotionally-driven decisions, if your intentions are fear-based, you need to learn how to manage those fears so that they do not dictate how you eventually handle your outcomes or situations (which could prevent you from making the right decisions for your desired outcomes.)

If your intentions happen to be fueled by anger or you have malicious intent, put a STOP to it immediately. Never intentionally make any type of decision(s) that you know may harm others.

TIP 32 | INTENTIONS FUEL MOTIVATIONS

Regardless of whatever rationale you may tell yourself to justify acting upon choices based in negativity, believe me, negativity begets negativity. Unhappy or unsuccessful people often try to intentionally undermine or unravel other people's success because they are often too afraid to either face, or deal with, their own insecurities and failure. This leads them to make repeatedly poor decisions where they remain captive in a negative vortex of their own creation.

However, most successful people do not pander to getting stuck in this negative quagmire. In order to avoid succumbing to making unproductive and negative decisions in the future, take that extra moment to simply <u>pause</u> and ask yourself:

- "What are my underlying intentions for making this decision?"

- "What reaction am I hoping to solicit from others?

- "How will I personally benefit/gain from the outcome of my decision?"

Let your intentions positively motivate you to achieve your desired outcomes for success!

Have you ever wondered what your rate of return (e.g., future reward or opportunities) might be for all of your hard work, time, and/or money that you have invested in a certain endeavor?

For example, a decision to invest in continuing education after you graduate college (certifications, seminars, workshops, educational bootcamps, etc.) could potentially help you to improve your knowledge, talents, and skills, which could lead to new or better personal and professional opportunities.

Before you make any future decisions, get into the habit of always taking a moment to pause and weigh whether your time, energy, and/or money will create any additional opportunities toward you achieving your desired outcomes for success.

TIP 33 "YOUR FUTURE SELF WILL THANK YOU"

Pause.

Then ask yourself:

"How will the outcome of my decision(s) enhance my future?"

Volunteering for an event, joining an organization, or interning for a company that interests you would qualify as a worthwhile way for you to spend your time and energy to receive a positive return on that investment. Not only would these situations create excellent opportunities for networking, collaborating, and meeting new people with similar interests, but they could also pave the way to creating opportunities for future growth.

Consider bartering...consulting or tutoring others in exchange for free referrals, references, or endorsements. On top of receiving "word of mouth" testimonials and/or referrals, you will likely find it very gratifying to help others with your unique talents. These exchanges will also add to your growing roster of new contacts and lead to new opportunities.

If America is truly the land of opportunity, then why can't everybody land their dream job or career after graduation? Are some young men and women just better at focusing their time and energy toward manifesting the job or career they desire? Do some graduates simply lack the ability to make positive strategic decisions that would allow them to acquire the job/careers they want?

I believe the answer to both is "yes." I believe the single greatest road to one's success is their commitment and ability to manifest and pursue a job or career that truly inspires their passion and desires.

TIP 34 | FOLLOW YOUR PASSION FOR SUCCESS

As you embark upon making life-changing decisions that could positively impact your abilities to land your ideal job/career, pause and carefully consider the following three criteria before you commit to any future jobs/careers:

1. **Quality of Life** — You should always do your best to find a job or career that will allow you to positively resonate both personally and professionally. Not only do you want to find (or start) a business that you would like to work for (or create), but you also want to

find a location (city, state, country, etc.) that you believe will best support your quality of life (natural pace and/or peace of mind).

2. **Challenge or Opportunity** — You should try to pursue a job or career that either challenges you, or provides you with opportunities to grow from the experience. So choose one that either serves as a stepping stone toward getting you your ultimate job/career, or choose a job/career that provides you with the opportunity to further educate yourself (new skills, talents, etc.), and/or supports your continued growth toward attaining your ideal outcome.

3. **Financial Reward** — Notice I listed this pursuit last? While I am all for finding a job/career path that monetarily rewards you for all of your hard work and efforts, I just don't believe money should be the sole driving force for choosing a job, business, or career. I think it should be viewed as a *tool for opportunity* — a financial means for continuing to invest in your future pursuits (passions/desires). I believe that the sooner one commits to living within their means, the money they end up being able to save up can enable and support them to pursue their ultimate goals.

Avoiding the "Freshman 15": Healthy Body, Healthy Mind

{Tips 35 – 39}

HEALTHY BODY, HEALTHY MIND

AVOIDING

HE WHO HAS HEALTH, HAS HOPE. AND HE WHO HAS HOPE, HAS EVERYTHING.

~ BENJAMIN FRANKLIN

the "FRESHMAN 15"

ACCORDING TO THE Center for Disease Control and Prevention (CDC), an estimated 17% of American children and young adults (ages 2-19) are now considered obese because they suffer from an imbalance between the calories they consume, and the calories they actually use (burning the calories off by metabolizing their caloric intake through physical activity). In other words, their food consumption (intake) outweighs their exercise levels (output). As a result, more and more younger (and older) adults are becoming more susceptible to acquiring life-threatening cardiovascular diseases (e.g., high blood pressure, high cholesterol, and type 2 diabetes).

Obesity amongst college graduates has not only become a health care epidemic, but it also poses a potential economic problem for prospective employers and companies. While I am not implying it is a legal practice, there may be an unspoken bias amongst some companies to avoid hiring obese employees due to their heightened risk of requiring extensive medical care which could potentially impact the company's fiscal bottom-line.

And to make matters worse, if the overweight or obese person does not reverse their condition early on, the costs of their potentially exorbitant medical bills could put their future retirement savings at risk (due to covering unplanned health-related problems out of pocket), potentially depleting one's retirement savings.

When it comes to your overall health, one cannot put a price tag on the TRUE costs associated with being hindered from performing everyday tasks and activities in life — quality of life is priceless.

Optimal physical health is more than just *appearing* fit — you've got to really *be* fit. There are plenty of out of shape average, or even thin, people whose health is compromised because they do not exercise (usually their "good genes" let them rest on their laurels).

If you want to avoid the all-too-common "Freshman 15" (the extra 15 pounds most freshman tack onto their waistlines after graduating high school) as a result of late night studying, partying, and over-indulging, then I cannot emphasize enough how important it will be to learn to con-sistently incorporate the following three deceptively simple health hab-its throughout your college years:

TIP 35 | YOUR OVERALL HEALTH

1. Exercise regularly

2. Eat/Drink healthily

3. Get plenty of sleep

Not only will living a healthy lifestyle help to make you feel good inside, but it will also continue to support your personal brand — because how you look on the outside most definitely is a reflection of how you feel on the inside.

For the next month, keep a log of:

- How often you exercise regularly (running, aerobics, cycling, etc.)

- Your current eating patterns (food/drink intake, AND the time of day you choose to eat and drink)

- How many hours you sleep each night (averaged).

Just as managing your study time is important to your overall collegiate success, managing your daily caloric intake is equally important to your overall health and well-being. It would be beneficial to consult with your personal doctor or nutritionist to help you determine the right amount of calories you should be consuming on a daily basis based upon your body size.

Here are some suggestions to help you manage your mindless (self-sabotaging) eating habits while studying or getting through your hectic college schedules:

TIP 36 | MANAGING YOUR INTAKE

1. **Find a free website or app that you can utilize to help you track and count your daily caloric intake.**

   Look for free sites or apps that provide healthy eating recipes or tips for staying healthy while on the go.

2. **Seek out community or online social media support groups.**

3. **Look for groups that will share blogs, message boards, articles, support, etc. to help you attain your healthy eating goals.**

4. **Try to balance your meals and limit un-healthy (possibly toxic) ingredients.**

   For example, excessive salt intake causes your body to bloat and retain water. Try to find healthy alternatives (pepper, spices, etc.). Drink lots of water or iced tea in place of carbonated soda, energy drinks, or other sweet beverages. (FYI, diet soda is not better for you than regular soda. In fact, the majority of them are loaded with artificial ingredients and there are many that argue diet sodas are actually detrimental to your good health.)

5. **When eating out, don't hesitate to request a "doggie bag" to go.**

   It is a well-known fact that American style restaurant portions are more than one needs to actually consume in one sitting. And as far as buffets or "family-style" dining goes...don't even get me started!

   Growing up, contrary to what you may have been programmed to believe, you <u>do</u> <u>not</u> need to eat all the food on your plate. Unfortunately people in the world will continue to starve whether or not you clean your plate. You will not alleviate world hunger.

There is no shame in telling your restaurant server you'd like to take your food "to go." It will taste just as good, if not better, at home, or back in your residence hall (especially when you're bogged down studying).

Think about and research the following, and take a few moments to write your responses:

Free Website or Smartphone Apps:

_____

Community Online or Social Media Support Groups:

_____

I will commit to replacing unhealthy beverages like soda, with healthy drinks like water at this/ these locations:

_____

How many meals per day: _____

How many days per week: _____

My final nutritional advice for helping you to avoid the "Freshman 15" involves residence hall living. Despite all the progress that is currently being made to offer healthier alternatives in resident hall dining facilities, many still cannot resist the urge to self-sabotage with fast, quick, on-the-go food choices.

To help you manage your potential fast-food sabotage, I highly recommend that you stock up on the following kinds of snacks in your resident hall room:

- nuts (almonds, walnuts...but avoid fattening peanuts)

TIP 37 | "BEHIND CLOSED DOORS"

- fruits (bananas, apples)

- vegetables (carrots, celery... avoid hard-to-digest corn)

- protein/energy bars (make sure to check the fat grams, sugar grams, and calorie content)

- string cheese, Greek yogurt, almond milk

Above all, remember this:
Everything in moderation!

If you have a roommate, or significant other, encourage each other to eat healthy foods. Keep each other accountable to make good food choices together that will allow you both to benefit from the results.

As I mentioned before, there is more to physical health than just *appearing* fit — you've got to *be* fit — there are plenty of out of shape, average, or even thin, people whose health is compromised because they do not exercise.

A strong body is a strong mind. You should try to find time to exercise at least three to four times per week, for at least a half-hour each day. Not only will regular exercise improve your confidence and personal brand, but it will also help clear your mind to make better decisions, thus improving your overall outlook on life.

TIP 38 | "THE ZIPPER NEVER LIES"

It is important that you discuss your plans for a new health regimen with a healthcare professional at your college's health center, a specialist at your university's gym, local health club, or your personal physician.

Not only will getting fit release a lot of tension and stress brought on by studying and college life in general, but you will also look and feel a whole lot stronger.

It is equally important that you give your body and mind the rest it needs because lack of sleep can increase weight gain.

If you ever watch weight loss TV shows like "The Biggest Loser," then you already know there are many options for achieving your overall health success. The important thing is to <u>decide</u> to change, <u>commit</u> to implementing that change, and then hold yourself <u>accountable</u> to achieving your desired results by addressing and removing any or all obstacles (including excuses, fears, etc.). Don't forget to utilize all the resources out there to your advantage. There are plenty of websites and apps that will help you to calculate and maintain a good goal weight (e.g., www.freebmicalculator) and exercise routines.

TIP 39 — "DECIDE, COMMIT, DON'T QUIT"

After first consulting with your healthcare specialist, here are three suggestions you could pursue for your new diet and exercise regimen:

1. To help you meet and maintain your fitness goals, commit to participating in fun, exercise-related activities that include: yoga, crossfit, bicycling, spinning, dancing, running, walking, martial arts, kickboxing, aerobics, cardio, or various collegiate intramural sports and activities. Most of these activities are usually offered on-campus, or less expensively through your local YMCA/YWCA.

2. Having others also invested in improving health and fitness along with you will help you take action and motivate yourself to stay accountable to your fitness goals. Consider working out with a "workout buddy" or group of supporters (friends, family, etc.) who will help push you to stay fit.

3. I highly recommend that you get at least seven – eight hours of sleep each night. Your body will tend to store up fat when you are tired and low on energy.

Rise to the challenge, support your strong personal brand, and begin your lifetime commitment to living a healthy lifestyle.

I am changing my exercise goals by <u>deciding</u> to:

_____

I am <u>committing</u> myself to exercising:

_____

I will hold myself <u>accountable</u> to my exercise goals by:

_____

MIRACLES SOMETIMES OCCUR, BUT ONE HAS TO WORK TERRIBLY HARD FOR THEM.

~ CHAIM WEIZMANN

Dollars and Sense: Kickstarting Your Financial Success

{Tips 40 – 45}

MONEY IS BETTER THAN POVERTY, IF ONLY FOR FINANCIAL REASONS.

~ WOODY ALLEN

KICKSTARTING YOUR FINANCIAL SUCCESS

DOLLARS AND SENSE

AS A YOUNG college student, I have to imagine that life in the 21st Century must seem pretty uncertain and somewhat scary to you right now. If it makes you feel any better, you're not alone. It has been well-documented that young adults are not only finding it increasingly difficult to obtain employment after graduating college, but they are also finding that their lack of financial education has left many of them ill-equipped to make good personal and financial decisions, which hinders their opportunities to become successful and financially independent.

The financial affliction from which so many American adults between the ages of 40 and 60 suffer ("financial obesity"), leaves them trapped in an unhealthy, self-sabotaging, and vicious cycle of living beyond their financial means. In much the same way one self-medicates through their addiction of choice, the financially obese are obsessive-compulsively driven to soothe themselves through their "drug" of choice — spending money they don't have in order to fill their emotional voids. Eventually, instead of the intended outcome of making themselves feel better, they ultimately end up feeling worse as they have financially starved themselves.

Don't get me wrong, I'm not implying that spending money is an unhealthy practice, but what *is* healthy is living within your financial means.

Your goal from this moment forward should be to avoid the current misconceptions regarding over-spending and poor money management that continue to plague so many older adults. By doing so, you will have given yourself the opportunity after graduation to become an excellent money manager and wealth creator.

To clarify my definition of personal finance (which encompasses both the value of, and one's strategic relationship with, money), from this moment forward, I think you might find it helpful to think of your own strategic relationship with money in terms of the following car/driving analogy:

Think of money like it's the gas pedal (accelerator) in your car. Just as you would apply pressure to your car's accelerator to make the car go faster, the more money that you save and invest will help you accelerate your financial goals more quickly. However, to achieve your financial success most effectively (the most direct route), you will need to manage your money efficiently by avoiding reckless spending.

TIP 40 | "DRIVING WITHIN YOUR FINANCIAL MEANS"

Just like reckless speeding can derail the driver, reckless spending can also result in serious financial and emotional setbacks. However, like an experienced safe driver, by being financially aware of your surroundings (your savings and spending habits) and always driving within your life's financial speed limits (living within your means), you will be creating the opportunity to acquire the financial freedom to really enjoy life's beautiful scenery (your family, friends, career, travel, etc.).

But before you can create your own newfound wealth, it is important for you to first be able to clearly define what wealth truly means to you.

Take a moment to jot down and define what you believe constitutes wealth? What does a wealthy person look like, or live like?

1 _____

_____

2 _____

_____

3 _____

_____

4 _____

_____

I used to ask myself, "Why would U.S. schools spend so much time, effort, and money to educate and test students on such important subjects such as math, English, history, science, language, etc. but then fail to teach their students anything regarding proper money management?" The politically correct answer: "Well, money is a personal subject, and therefore finances should really be discussed in the home between children and their parents." The more probable reason why most schools do not teach students about personal finance or money management: There is no universal or formally accepted educational model to teach them about the value of, or more importantly, one's strategic relationship with money.

TIP 41

WHAT IS YOUR EMOTIONAL RELATIONSHIP WITH MONEY?

As you may have observed, people tend to have their own personal relationship with money, just like they do with other personal things in their life (e.g., people, food, fear, risk, etc.). However, the way most people tend to learn about, and develop their own relationship with money is often based upon their own early childhood programming by having observed their parents, teachers, friends, and/or the media. For example, you may have heard someone projecting their own personal relationship with money (values) on others by making generalizations along the lines of, "That Robert is way too conservative for me!" Or, "Look at that Jennifer, she spends like there is no tomorrow!" These generalizations tend to be a reflection of one's *parents'* relationship with money. So, let's say your parents are, or were, conservative with money, and you embraced that value. Then you will most likely follow suit and be more conservative with your own money. However, if you disliked the way your parents either frugally saved, or recklessly overspent their money, then you might ultimately decide to manage your own money the opposite way.

Before you can establish your own definition for wealth, you must first acknowledge and embrace your own strategic relationship with money. How would you describe your relationship with money?

_____

_____

_____

As I said earlier, most young adults tend to learn their good or bad saving/spending habits by observing their parents, friends, etc. This early exposure often dictates how most children will either emotionally, or strategically, manage their relationship with money as an adult. Will they be confident, fearful, frugal, thrifty, etc.? When one has an unhealthy emotional relationship with money, it becomes the catalyst for so many "financial obesity" issues.

Here are a couple of basic money management techniques and strategies to help you better understand wealth creation, while also helping you to avoid self-sabotaging financial obesity:

TIP 42 | HOW TO AVOID "FINANCIAL OBESITY"

1. **Are you clueless about your current spending?**

   To help you get a better grip on why your current cash flow never seems to be flowing, start writing down and tracking all of your daily expenses (how much you are actually spending each day) in a small notebook. Write down the date, place, and exact amount you spend on each and every expense so that you can visually track and understand where all of your money is going. After compiling all this new information, take it a step further, and create a monthly spending budget so you can keep better track of where your money is being spent, and more importantly, on what?!

If you would like to learn more about these money saving techniques, pick up a copy of my book, *Demystifying Success: Success Tools and Secrets They Don't Teach You in High School.*

2. **Save at least 10% of your monthly income in a personal savings account.**

Get in the habit **now** of saving (i.e., putting away) $0.10 for every dollar that you potentially earn from this moment forward into an interest bearing personal savings or money market account.

Your future self will thank you!

Whenever we hear the term "debt," we usually associate it with negative stereotypes such as, "He owes a lot of debt," or "She is in way over her head in debt." However, most successful wealth creators actually learn how to manage two different types of debt — good debt and bad debt.

If you find yourself either purchasing or acquiring some product/service that requires you to borrow money from a lender with interest (additional charges), and this product/service never generates any probable passive income (profit) for you in the future, that's <u>bad</u> <u>debt</u>.

TIP 43 | BAD DEBT VERSUS GOOD DEBT

Here's a hypothetical example: Suppose you are watching late-night TV, and you see a product being sold on an infomercial and in that moment you emotionally decide that you *must* have this product **now**. The only problem is, this "must have" product does not offer a payment plan, and will cost $500 (which you do not currently have). But wait…you *must* have it! So in the heat of the moment, you come up with an easy (emotional) solution to get what you want. You will simply charge this amazing product (on one of your high-interest credit cards) so that there will be no delay in receiving it. When the product arrives a few days later, you get some instant gratification. Then, about a month later, the credit card bill arrives.

The following three tips will help you avoid accruing additional bad debt (i.e., fees/penalties):

1. **Pay off your outstanding balances (in full)** — If you must charge any items on credit cards, make sure to pay off all outstanding balances the very next month to avoid getting stuck in the expensive cycle of paying the monthly compounded interest rate fees (and additional late fees [if you don't make your payments on time]). If you find that you are unable to pay off all of your outstanding balances within a month, that's a sign that you are probably using credit cards as "extended income," and that you should not be using credit whatsoever (especially not for impulsive emotional purchases).

2. **Pay your credit card balances, loans, and other expenses on time** — Create a calendar alert or buy yourself a monthly planner or wall calendar so that you can write the full, or minimum amounts due, as well as the due dates owed to each company. This will ensure that you don't miss your monthly payment. For example: $25.00 due to MasterCard® on August

14th. Make sure you always get your payments credited to your credit card, loan, etc. accounts <u>by</u> their stated due date. Each month your bill arrives, make sure you pay careful attention to the actual due dates printed on the statement as these dates may fluctuate. Credit card bills are due every 30 days from the billing cycle date — not necessarily the same date each month (based upon their 30-day billing cycle contractual fine print).

3. **Protect your FICO score** — Your ability to manage your credit obligations (good and bad credit) is determined by a score, which is called your <u>FICO</u> score. "FICO" is an acronym for the Fair Isaac Company which was named after the company that first created and computed this standardized credit score. Each month, lending institutions and credit card companies report your payment history to three different credit rating agencies: Equifax, Experian, and TransUnion. In turn, these three credit rating agencies supply lenders with your FICO score. Your FICO score can range from 300 (poor) to 850 (excellent).

When borrowing money to make major purchases (house, car, boat, etc.), the higher your FICO score, the better "deal" a lending institution may offer by giving you a lower interest rate for the life of the loan. The lower your FICO score (the closer you get to 300), the higher credit risk you become to the lenders, thereby diminishing your chances of being offered any credit whatsoever.

What I am about to say next may seem inconsistent with what I have just shared with you; not all debt should be perceived as "bad debt." For example, when depositing money you are the one actually loaning the bank money and in return, the bank pays you interest on that money (albeit at a much lower interest rate than the credit card/loan companies would charge you). Additionally, it's not always considered bad debt to borrow money from a bank, investor, or even a credit card company if you strategically plan to use the borrowed money to purchase things that will increase your bottom line (profits) in the future. This type of debt is usually called "good debt" because the potentially positive outcome is considered great enough that it outweighs the cost of the interest you pay on the borrowed money.

For example, if you take out a mortgage to purchase real estate with the intent to charge others rent for occupancy, then you are applying the borrowed money toward an investment expected to generate revenue (profits) in the future. Ultimately, carrying that good debt can be justified as a means to a profitable end — paying the mortgage off in full to own the property outright, while continuing to collect passive rental income.

The following are examples where other debt may be incurred (e.g., fees/penalties) and also associated with "<u>good debt</u>":

- Borrowing money to start a new business or entrepreneurial venture

- Borrowing to reinvest money into a current business in order to grow the business' inventory, supplies, machinery, advertising, development, etc.

However, I do <u>not</u> recommend that you <u>ever</u> borrow money to invest in the stock market (even if you try justifying it by thinking you can get a return on that investment). Unlike investing in your own business, not only could you lose money in the stock market, but you will still be obligated to pay back the initial borrowed money — with interest.

In case you ever need to rely on credit to grow your good debt (securing real estate loans), and you put charges on your credit cards, stay vigilant in protecting your high FICO score. Pay all monthly due balances on time — <u>by</u> their stated due dates.

Understanding and maintaining a positive strategic relationship with money is crucial in helping you establish more responsible spending habits that will lead you to growing your savings.

If you find that you tend to be especially vulnerable to your "wants" versus your "needs" in trying to "keep up with the Joneses" (pressure you may feel from the influences of the media or from having adopted others' negative relationships with money), then you will definitely need to begin practicing disciplined spending restraint. Keep your emotional spending in check to make sure you always live within your financial means. As a future wealth creator, to help you remain disciplined toward building a solid financial foundation for your long-term wealth and success, before you ever open your wallet and reach for your cash or credit cards (or if you're shopping online, hit that "buy it now" button linked to your credit or PayPal account), take a moment to pause... think...and check in with your better instincts. If you feel any moment of hesitation, you can bet that your impulsive "must have" purchase will most likely never benefit you in the long run.

TIP 44 | "KEEPING UP WITH THE JONESES"

To help ensure that you always live within your financial means, I have designed the following questions to guide you in making good strategic (non-emotional) purchasing decisions:

1. **What is the *probability* that your purchasing decision will lead to a successful outcome, and how will this product or service get you any closer to achieving your overall personal or financial goals?**

   This would be a good time to step back and honestly ask yourself if purchasing this product or service would really be a good strategic decision, rather than merely trying to justify a "want" to yourself or to please someone else by making some emotionally-driven purchase.

2. **How will this purchase ultimately benefit you personally, and/or professionally?**

   Do not allow yourself to feel guilty or manipulated into making any purchases that you may later regret. If you are not sure how you can immediately benefit, go ahead and sleep on it — don't rush your decisions. Always remember that old adage that if something is too good to be true, it usually is.

3. **How long do I plan to use this product or service before it becomes obsolete?**

   Is there a predetermined time limit on how long you can utilize this product or service? What is your exit strategy if this purchase does not deliver the results you had anticipated when you purchased it?

4. **What additional opportunities will this purchase provide for me?**

   What reaction are you hoping to solicit from others or benefit/gain from purchasing this product or service?

5. **What would happen if I chose to wait another two to six months until I could honestly afford to make this purchase without having to borrow any money?**

   Would you really miss some important opportunity, or does it make more sense for you to not go into debt by borrowing money (credit or loan) at this time? What would the consequence(s) be if you just gave yourself more time to simply pause and sleep on it?

   By continuing to ask yourself "why" when choosing to make future purchasing decisions, you will not only be developing new positive spending habits, but you will also be helping ensure that your decisions align with your intentions and desired outcomes.

Because no one has — or ever will — care more about your money than you do, you need to start taking responsibility for your long-term financial future — today — because the cavalry ain't coming. No one knows what the future will hold for them. So without a crystal ball, you need to start thinking about your old age <u>now</u> in order to be well-prepared for the unknown. Let's review what we *do* know about the future:

- We know that the Social Security Retirement Trust Fund is expected to run out by 2034

TIP 45 | THE CAVALRY AIN'T COMING

- We also know that no one should really rely on their company or country to bail them out or take care of them in their old age

So, why does this pertain to *you*, right now? Because, as a young college student, you have one major **advantage** going for you that a lot of older adults don't: <u>TIME</u>!

Since it is never too early to <u>kick-start</u> your retirement planning, I would like to share **five basic tips to help you begin thinking about saving for your retirement:**

1. **Start saving a percentage of your monthly income in a personal savings account (preferably at least 10%)** — This money should only be used for emergencies. Remember, this is not an extension of your checking account so resist the temptation to treat it like an ATM — leave it alone and let it continue to grow.

2. **Create and manage a monthly spending budget** — Learning to live within your budget is crucial in helping you prepare for retirement. The money you begin saving and growing for your retirement should last you a long time (dependent, of course, upon your life expectancy). Learning to budget and manage your money, early on, will help ensure that you have enough money to live off of throughout your retirement years.

3. **Open a standard IRA, and/or contribute to your company's 401(k) program** — Not only are these plans tax-deferred, but if invested properly, they will grow by compounding your annual rate of return. The earlier you start, the more opportunity your retirement money will grow over time. Don't let the decades fly by (ask any elderly person, they really do!) and wake up one day wishing you had been more prepared for retirement.

4. **Always live within your means** — Make sure to pay off all of your credit card balances on time. Avoid incurring any large balances that will require you to pay a lot of interest (additional cost) on your purchases (i.e., bad debt). If you cannot afford to pay off your entire credit card balance within a month or two of your purchase, then consider delaying your purchase(s) until you can <u>afford</u> to cover your expenses. Again, live within your means and protect your FICO credit score, as your money management impacts your ability to borrow money in the future, as well as plan for retirement.

5. **Always take preventative health measures** — As we discussed, continue to eat healthily and exercise regularly so that you can avoid any serious or major medical expenses that can either exhaust your retirement savings, or derail your retirement plans altogether in your old age. Ultimately, if you don't have your good health, you are missing out on one of your greatest assets.

By learning how to become financially literate, from an early age, you will establish life-long wealth-generating habits to help enable you to successfully retire comfortably, confidently, and with peace of mind.

THE MOST IMPORTANT THING YOU CAN DO TO ACHIEVE YOUR GOALS IS TO MAKE SURE THAT AS SOON AS YOU SET THEM, YOU IMMEDIATELY BEGIN TO CREATE MOMENTUM.

~ TONY ROBBINS

Calls to *Action*

{Freshman – Senior+ years}

{1} Mentors

1| _____
_____
2| _____
_____
3| _____
_____
4| _____
_____
5| _____
_____

{2} Network, Network, Network

1| _____
_____
2| _____
_____
3| _____
_____
4| _____
_____
5| _____
_____

{3} Healthy Personal Relationships

1| _____
_____
2| _____
_____
3| _____
_____
4| _____
_____
5| _____
_____

{4} Be Distinct Or Be Extinct

1| _____
_____
2| _____
_____
3| _____
_____
4| _____
_____
5| _____
_____

{5} Time Management: Successful Study Secrets and Tips

1| _____
_____
2| _____
_____
3| _____
_____
4| _____
_____
5| _____
_____

{ NOTES }

{ 6 } From the Classroom to the Boardroom

1| _____
_____
2| _____
_____
3| _____
_____
4| _____
_____
5| _____
_____

{ 7 } Dreams are for Bedtime, Goals are for Success!

1| _____
_____
2| _____
_____
3| _____
_____
4| _____
_____
5| _____
_____

{ 8 } The Art of the Pause

1| _____
_____
2| _____
_____
3| _____
_____
4| _____
_____
5| _____
_____

{ 9 } Avoiding the "Freshman 15"

1| _____
_____
2| _____
_____
3| _____
_____
4| _____
_____
5| _____
_____

{ 10 } Dollars and Sense

1| _____
_____
2| _____
_____
3| _____
_____
4| _____
_____
5| _____
_____

{ NOTES }

{1} Mentors

1| _____
_____

2| _____
_____

3| _____
_____

4| _____
_____

5| _____
_____

{2} Network, Network, Network

1| _____
_____

2| _____
_____

3| _____
_____

4| _____
_____

5| _____
_____

{3} Healthy Personal Relationships

1| _____
_____

2| _____
_____

3| _____
_____

4| _____
_____

5| _____
_____

{4} Be Distinct Or Be Extinct

1| _____
_____

2| _____
_____

3| _____
_____

4| _____
_____

5| _____
_____

{5} Time Management: Successful Study Secrets and Tips

1| _____
_____

2| _____
_____

3| _____
_____

4| _____
_____

5| _____
_____

{ NOTES }

Sophomore year

{ 6 }
From the Classroom to the Boardroom

1| _____

_____

2| _____

_____

3| _____

_____

4| _____

_____

5| _____

_____

{ 7 }
Dreams are for Bedtime, Goals are for Success!

1| _____

_____

2| _____

_____

3| _____

_____

4| _____

_____

5| _____

_____

{ 8 }
The Art of the Pause

1| _____

_____

2| _____

_____

3| _____

_____

4| _____

_____

5| _____

_____

{ 9 }
Avoiding the "Freshman 15"

1| _____

_____

2| _____

_____

3| _____

_____

4| _____

_____

5| _____

_____

{ 10 }
Dollars and Sense

1| _____

_____

2| _____

_____

3| _____

_____

4| _____

_____

5| _____

_____

{ NOTES }

_____

_____

_____

_____

_____

_____

_____

{1}
Mentors

1|_____
_____
2|_____
_____
3|_____
_____
4|_____
_____
5|_____
_____

{2}
Network,
Network,
Network

1|_____
_____
2|_____
_____
3|_____
_____
4|_____
_____
5|_____
_____

{3}
Healthy
Personal
Relationships

1|_____
_____
2|_____
_____
3|_____
_____
4|_____
_____
5|_____
_____

{4}
Be Distinct Or
Be Extinct

1|_____
_____
2|_____
_____
3|_____
_____
4|_____
_____
5|_____
_____

{5}
Time Management:
Successful Study
Secrets and Tips

1|_____
_____
2|_____
_____
3|_____
_____
4|_____
_____
5|_____
_____

{ NOTES }

{ 6 }
From the Classroom to the Boardroom

1| _____
_____
2| _____
_____
3| _____
_____
4| _____
_____
5| _____
_____

{ 7 }
Dreams are for Bedtime, Goals are for Success!

1| _____
_____
2| _____
_____
3| _____
_____
4| _____
_____
5| _____
_____

{ 8 }
The Art of the Pause

1| _____
_____
2| _____
_____
3| _____
_____
4| _____
_____
5| _____
_____

{ 9 }
Avoiding the "Freshman 15"

1| _____
_____
2| _____
_____
3| _____
_____
4| _____
_____
5| _____
_____

{ 10 }
Dollars and Sense

1| _____
_____
2| _____
_____
3| _____
_____
4| _____
_____
5| _____
_____

{ NOTES }

{1}
Mentors

1|_____
_____
2|_____
_____
3|_____
_____
4|_____
_____
5|_____
_____

{2}
Network,
Network,
Network

1|_____
_____
2|_____
_____
3|_____
_____
4|_____
_____
5|_____
_____

{3}
Healthy
Personal
Relationships

1|_____
_____
2|_____
_____
3|_____
_____
4|_____
_____
5|_____
_____

{4}
Be Distinct Or
Be Extinct

1|_____
_____
2|_____
_____
3|_____
_____
4|_____
_____
5|_____
_____

{5}
Time Management:
Successful Study
Secrets and Tips

1|_____
_____
2|_____
_____
3|_____
_____
4|_____
_____
5|_____
_____

{ NOTES }

Senior year

{ 6 }
From the Classroom to the Boardroom

1|_____
_____
2|_____
_____
3|_____
_____
4|_____
_____
5|_____
_____

{ 7 }
Dreams are for Bedtime, Goals are for Success!

1|_____
_____
2|_____
_____
3|_____
_____
4|_____
_____
5|_____
_____

{ 8 }
The Art of the Pause

1|_____
_____
2|_____
_____
3|_____
_____
4|_____
_____
5|_____
_____

{ 9 }
Avoiding the "Freshman 15"

1|_____
_____
2|_____
_____
3|_____
_____
4|_____
_____
5|_____
_____

{ 10 }
Dollars and Sense

1|_____
_____
2|_____
_____
3|_____
_____
4|_____
_____
5|_____
_____

{ NOTES }

Call to *Action*

{1}
Mentors

1|_____
_____
2|_____
_____
3|_____
_____
4|_____
_____
5|_____
_____

{2}
Network,
Network,
Network

1|_____
_____
2|_____
_____
3|_____
_____
4|_____
_____
5|_____
_____

{3}
Healthy
Personal
Relationships

1|_____
_____
2|_____
_____
3|_____
_____
4|_____
_____
5|_____
_____

{4}
Be Distinct Or
Be Extinct

1|_____
_____
2|_____
_____
3|_____
_____
4|_____
_____
5|_____
_____

{5}
Time Management:
Successful Study
Secrets and Tips

1|_____
_____
2|_____
_____
3|_____
_____
4|_____
_____
5|_____
_____

{ NOTES }

{ 6 } From the Classroom to the Boardroom

1|_____
_____
2|_____
_____
3|_____
_____
4|_____
_____
5|_____
_____

{ 7 } Dreams are for Bedtime, Goals are for Success!

1|_____
_____
2|_____
_____
3|_____
_____
4|_____
_____
5|_____
_____

{ 8 } The Art of the Pause

1|_____
_____
2|_____
_____
3|_____
_____
4|_____
_____
5|_____
_____

{ 9 } Avoiding the "Freshman 15"

1|_____
_____
2|_____
_____
3|_____
_____
4|_____
_____
5|_____
_____

{ 10 } Dollars and Sense

1|_____
_____
2|_____
_____
3|_____
_____
4|_____
_____
5|_____
_____

{ NOTES }